Nectar of Fermented Mind

Nectar of
Fermented Mind

CARMINE PARI

Also by
Carmine Pari

NO MORE TIME: Selected Stories (2015)

CONTENTS

VERSE · 1
GODDESS · 2
FATHER · 3
LAST KISS · 4
SKEPTIC · 5
My words are dead · 6
SAND CASTLES · 7
COMMERCE · 8
While playing his flute · · · · · · · · · · · · · · · · · · · 9
MOUNTAINS · 10
TOMBED TOWN ·11
The choice was never mine · · · · · · · · · · · · · · 12
DEPARTEE · 13
CROW TO PARROTS · 14
how beautiful my tree · · · · · · · · · · · · · · · · · · 16
Questions big · 17
A MASTER · 18
BOOKWORM · 19

TERRARIUM · 20

Sleeping beneath stars · · · · · · · · · · · · · · · · · 22

NO MORE TIME · 23

FINAL MOMENT · 24

A bumblebee flies · 25

POESY · 26

HERO · 28

Written with my blood · · · · · · · · · · · · · · · · · · 29

ANGEL · 30

Pines and firs in fall · 31

HOME · 32

Anticipating · 33

DAWN · 34

MEMORIAL · 36

Bombs fall from dark clouds · · · · · · · · · · · · · 37

OUR BROTHER'S KEEPER · · · · · · · · · · · · · · · 38

The sound of a stream · · · · · · · · · · · · · · · · · · 39

INFERTILE · 40

My secret · 41

FINAL FRIEND · 42

Thunder and lightening · · · · · · · · · · · · · · · · · 43

TREE · 44

Not through good or love · · · · · · · · · · · · · · · · 45

LINES · 46

INSIGNIFICANCE · 47

You know plants · 48

You get more with money · · · · · · · · · · · · · · · · 49

THE GREATEST GOD · 50
On a sultry night · 51
Standing in its waves · 52
From a mountaintop · 53
An eagle in flight · 54
White-feathered eagle · 55
Breathing in the scents · 56
Old pond · 57
A praying mantis · 58
PREYERS · 59
DAMNED · 60
ALMS FOR THE BLIND · 62
HUMANS · 63
There once was a man in love · · · · · · · · · · · · · · · · · 64
There once was a thief on the run · · · · · · · · · · · · · · · 65
There once was man who was poor · · · · · · · · · · · · · · 66
There once was a man from Nantucket · · · · · · · · · · · · 67
There once was a priest with regret · · · · · · · · · · · · · · 68
During Roman times · 69
I feel Death's grip inside my chest, · · · · · · · · · · · · · · · 70
MIMIC · 71
BELLETRIST · 72
CANDID DELUSION · 73
CONFIRMATION · 74
Re · 75
JUDGEMENT · 76
Old cheating box · 77

LOVE TO HATE · 78
LIES · 79
AN AWAKENING · 80
BONES · 81
A body · 82
Bye family and friends · 83
JUST MATTER · 84
On a hot sidewalk · 85
PARALLEL · 86
POST · 87
ATHEIST · 88
POEM? · 89
Reaching down to help · 90
BEST · 91
BEAUTY ON THE LAWN · 92
We walk the woods · 94
SKELETONS · 95
MACHINE · 96
ENDANGERED SPECIES · 97
OUR LAST WORDS · 98
HANGING A GOD · 99
COMPUTER VERSE · 100
TIME · 101
No recollection · 102
From our creator · 103
Worshiping on knee · 104
Blest wars in His name · 105

Standing on a cliff · 106
DEAD ALONE · 107
CLIFF · 108
A bullet in hand · 109
HOPE ·110
Eight plague on mankind ·111
A hero is made ·112
ASK ·113
ANGEL'S LAST DAY ·114
In my mirror I ·117
Beautiful last night ·118
No job ·119
Fists against his head · 120
Art is relative ·121
Holding her in bed · 122
Drifts alone at sea · 123
Stumbling through the door · · · · · · · · · · · · · · · · · ·124
Old pond reappears · 125
Smiling and waving · 126
A lone swimmer strokes · 127
Yearning bud of love · 128
Acorn falls from branch · 129
Where to rest one's head · · · · · · · · · · · · · · · · · · · 130
Walking in New York ·131
Hiking through thick woods · · · · · · · · · · · · · · · · · · 132
Pellets bang through mist · · · · · · · · · · · · · · · · · · · 133
Waking in a bed · 134

Playing hide-and-seek · 135
Naked at the stove · 136
A joke said at dawn ·137
They bow then fight · 138
Everyone lying · 139
Tall green roadside firs · 140
DEATH ·141
FINAL PRAYER · 142
WITNESS · 144
CERBERUS · 146
Our prisons house some ·147
SLEEPER · 148
OLD · 150
In a verdant vale ·151
ILLICIT BEAUTY · 152
Life · 153
THIRD · 154
It's just war · 155
GODS · 156
They choose · 157
LIFE · 158
Not mine. ·159
CIVILIZED · 160
MOUNTAIN GIANTS ·161
t. · 162
We always have · 163
HELP · 164
I CARE · 165

FOR GOD'S SAKE · 166
LI ·167
Hare running on snow · 168
NOTICE-ME SYNDROME · · · · · · · · · · · · · · · · · · ·169
Human life ·170

VERSE

Stressed feet that beat across the leaves,
Eyed from the west and to the east,
Pressed onto flat and white dead trees,
Dark prints that mark a poet's way.

GODDESS

Clear goddess who rules the sun god by force,
Where you reside is still a mystery,
Shined lenses search the heavens for your source,
Olympus or another galaxy.

'Twas you and not the sun that pulled him down,
For not respecting your attractive gift,
Winged Icarus from sky to sea to drown,
'Cause you control all matter that we lift.

We breathe because of your expansive touch,
Despite its felt invisibility,
Earth-stabilizing presence like a crutch,
Famed law that drops an apple from a tree.

Thus for your sustenance we daily pray,
Our deaths will surely come if you decay.

FATHER

I see your face, your many faces flat
I see the numbers we agree are you

A father watching me throughout my life
But of your true self, Father, I do not see you
I feel that you do not see me

I wish to better understand you
I want to walk with you when you were young
And dream of seeing you when you are old

You can be helpful, or you can bring woes
So sometimes we are friends and sometimes foes

My father of imagination

LAST KISS

I kissed and hugged my dearest friend,
My last before my nearing end,
And wiped away my tears of pain,
Not knowing if we'd meet again.

SKEPTIC

Alone, in the dark of night, I listen
And hear
What was told and what is told.

And in the quiet, I look
And see
What was written and what is written.

I doubt my senses,
For I am deaf and blind
To what they heard and saw,
And what they hear and see.

I doubt
I am wrong
When alone.

My words are dead
If they're not read
And understood
And so am I

SAND CASTLES

He often traveled to the beach
And found sand castles still survived
Despite dark confusion
And crashing waves.

In the bright light
Of a new day,
He swam in ocean waves
And saw sand castles rise
From countless grains of sand
Of unending creative beach.

He swam faster,
And the towers of sand castles
Rose higher into conception
And into the revealing heavens
That opened to allow expression
Of sand castles never seen
By him or anyone.

He dove deep into the black water
To reach the limit of ability,
To reach the source of sand castles,
And gasped at the miracles he birthed.

COMMERCE

Protecting female honor,
Her honey granted you,
Will earn more nights of commerce,
A payment offered few.

Once coupled in the dark,
The business tween you two,
In public cease remark,
A chivalrous ado.

When asked the inappropriate,
About her birds and bees,
The secret you must not reveal,
Imply she is a tease.

While playing his flute
He hears a sweeter player
A finch on a wire

❧

MOUNTAINS

One mountain saw and heard
Another mountain far off,
Could see the trees sway
On the mountain, sway from
The wind, and heard
The sounds of the wind.

The one mountain believed
It knew, understood,
The movements and sounds
From other mountains.

But distance between mountains is
Always vast, insurmountable,
No matter how close mountains are together,
Or seem to be.
No two mountains ever become one.

TOMBED TOWN

Can't rest in peace in my tombed town,
A plotted space to see,
My family dear and neighbors known
Are sleeping nearby me.

No more than just a putrid hole,
A needless dwelling mere,
No sanity, just haunted soul,
Remains of faithful sere.

In prison snug where I can't see,
Boxed deep in dark alone,
I wait the Shepherd's love decree,
Blest Son whose word is sown.

An angel's voice and trump of God
Will herald rapture earned,
Then from my dust He'll raise my bod
To live in heaven yearned.

The choice was never mine
To be or not to be
Before I breathed the life
My parents gave to me.

DEPARTEE

A Nile of vital red cut free,
Life giving source of me,
Spills in a porcelain walled sea
To drain the departee.

The fractured psyche, pray drugs ban,
An ancient plague to man,
Caused me first born, with blade in hand,
To damn the flesh to sand.

I planned my words be found too late,
By those I love and hate,
No longer burden, friend or foe,
True why will cause them woe.

CROW TO PARROTS

Why are you screaming!
Screams of alarm?
Is the sky falling,
The sun struggling to rise?

You woke me
Heralds of light,
Trumps of continuation
Of life,

Jolted me
From lid-closed height
At termination of
Wing-cold night.

We still live!
Your squawks rage,
As if clipped behind a cage,
And I caw fair warning back,

All clothed in integrating black.
What do you want,
Why have you come,
Here, where free breed,

In cantankerous concord,
Disturbing earned peace
Of diverse colonizers,
Their descendants, assimilators?

You camouflaged intruders,
Uninvited guests,
Your masses invading
With beating swiftness,

Why do you hide
Behind the leaves,
Blending, unseen,
Green behind green?

Share our fruits,
Live in our trees,
But do so calmly,
I bid you, please.

how beautiful my tree
a tree like many
grown from seeds
from trees
of countries overseas
not lived by me
but by my family

Questions big
Answers small
Honest words
Man's heart's call

A MASTER

you looking down upon my prose,
a witness to how my pen flows,
to justly judge if my art grows,

i try to write as masters do,
sage words on paper read as true,

fight to create my aging best,
work days and nights with little rest,
and dream that I might pass your test,

so by their tomes and leaves I wait,
and wonder what will be my fate,

if like them I will be a master,
and be remembered ever after,
or be laughed at and thought a jester!

BOOKWORM

With table and candle, fat in a seat,
It treats its hunger, looking for meat.
To sate its cravings, glasses it needs,
For Homer and Bible, on both it feeds.

TERRARIUM

Manna falls,
A live young mouse,
From bright light

To the scorpion
That scurries back
To solid air

While breathy breeze
That blows
In times to bleed

Pulses space again
And carries stench
Of burning flesh,

And the tree branch shakes
As the sand quakes
To force the scorpion to sting.

Jab! Jab!
It must obey,
Must kill,

Upon the rock,
To appease the creature
Presiding above.

Unable to run
Or hide,
Walled in Moriah,

The scorpion stabs
Its stinger into
The helpless sacrifice.

The youth screeches
And writhes,
Heaves and dies.

Loud cheers!
The scorpion hears,
Unintelligible sounds,

But the creature
Will leave, and return
Again when

Manna drops
And the scorpion
Must kill.

Sleeping beneath stars
Vast minds dream in dark space
Hearts beat together

NO MORE TIME

a single lamp casts a gloomy, yellow haze
in our bedroom as I stare at the clock.

it is late, and time is long and slow
and weighing on me.

she will come home around dawn,
smelling of booze and sex,

and she will understand why I did it.
i guess what her reaction will be.

i pick up the gun—it is cold and heavy—
and I tremble to rest it against my head.

i cry, knowing the last thing I will hear
will be my sobbing,

and the last thing I will feel
will be my tears

dripping down my face.
to myself, I say, "Good-bye."

FINAL MOMENT

It is late,
It is quiet,
And I am alone

As I stare
At the clock
On the wall,

Wondering
Will I sense the moment,
Will I know the moment,

Fear the moment,
Accept the moment,
Then awake—anew?

A bumblebee flies
Among flowers in a field
Spreading life with buzz

POESY

Heavenly or worldly
Literally and enigmatic
A slave to its creators

Loved or disregarded
Measured and stressed
Ancient to today and tomorrow

Life splintered or woven
With Zeus and Yahweh
Death and murder embraced

Sights of Spring and Fall
Blossom to carcass odors
A touch of lace or bark

Desert quiet to city loud
Lemon and honey sensed
Bodily or imagined

Two legs and spider or worm
All breathing or dead and both
One world or another

Have been and will be
Not thought of yet
Chemical and electrical flows

Seen and heard
Burned or worshipped
Trash or awarded prizes

Known by all
And many practice
Its masters are few

HERO

I rest now as a hero in the light,
My brothers sleep beside me in the dark,
'Cause I turned coward and refused to fight,
And they found courage as they hit their mark.

What happened here my words can only tell,
Tales by my brothers stay right where they lie,
Of how I sent our enemies to hell,
And how my brothers bravely chanced to die.

It matters not my story be exact,
I hid so I could fight another day,
What comforts people is it seem a fact,
And ran when enemies began to slay.

For much of what we hear of war is myth,
War's witnessed truths we could not bear live with.

Written with my blood
You see only the black ink
My words on paper

ANGEL

When life seems lost in lonely thought
And all your prayers have come to naught
A friend might come that you will know
To guide you to where all must go

Pines and firs in fall
Lack leaves of sundry colors
Yet are green in snow

HOME

My home is much a mental cage,
To ponder sins we do,
Ill hid behind pained flesh and lids,
Freaks dreadful rage like flu.

I live in here and not out there,
Because of fear of you,
Locked down upon debated page,
Released in words to rue.

I see no chance life pardons me,
Like you my evil reigns,
And seek a time to wreak revenge,
Pen banes for human brains.

Anticipating
Childhood joys of skipping
Flat stones on a lake

DAWN

At first light, a yellow chick ran
Out from its coop for the first time
And onto the farmyard

Where it began to peck and eat
The feed spread out on the ground
Until a green mantis stood to face it,

A mantis armed to fight,
Its arms reaching and contracting,
Attacking the yellow chick.

So the yellow chick ran
And came to a brown gecko
That whipped the yellow chick's foot.

Then the yellow chick ran,
And ran into a gray mouse
That bit the yellow chick's toe.

And the yellow chick ran
Until it saw a pink earthworm wriggling in the dirt.
Curious, the yellow chick ran

To the worm, and minded
The worm wriggle,
And the yellow chick did not run.

The yellow chick pecked
The wriggling worm,
Pecked off a piece of the worm's flesh.

Tasting the worms blood and meat,
The chick pecked the worm to pieces
And swallowed them.

Then the chick ran,
With emergent pluck,
Ran back to the mantis.

MEMORIAL

Oh, my monument, our great sitter
Of justice in our land,
You would recognize the times
As being like those of your days,
It is sad to say in many ways,
Concerns and troubles the same
And causing the same,
Disobedience, uprisings, hatred,
And war, looming, again,
But maybe another you will be,
Be assassinated before it begins.

Bombs fall from dark clouds
Pelting men with stormy rain
Sons die in red mud

OUR BROTHER'S KEEPER

We came upon him
Breathing and bleeding
In the wayside dirt
As we trudged on

Through the mud and fog;
I wanted to pick him up,
Carry him,
But I feared

I too was weak
And would fall myself
And die
In this hellhole.

I threw our brother
A fish,
And we all left him
Behind with our fear.

The sound of a stream
Singing silence to a bird
Sleeping in a tree

INFERTILE

In spring a blossom yearned to thrive,
By summer earned no peat to wive,
With fertile root, no flower bloomed,
While waiting, wanting, lust consumed;

The fruit it eyed it could not buy,
As passing time caused seeds to die;
Retarding autumn raised regret,
For sprouts not born, could not forget;

The fear of winter's touch was clear,
As eve of life grew ever near,
Though hope remained, soul not yet claimed,
For pined-for buds it never named.

My secret
Secrets
Scare me

FINAL FRIEND

Kin whisper of your coming,
Believing I can't hear,
My final absolution,
A priest is kneeling near.

You visit all but once,
Bestow the parting kiss,
To souls that must succumb,
That preachers say brings bliss.

I pray now for your mercy,
Bones shaded under hood,
Like many who await you,
Have faith you foretell good.

Thunder and lightening
In a storm of rain and wind
Mountains cradling trees

TREE

When once I came upon the tree
Quite quietly it spoke with me
Revealing secrets I would know
From where lives flow and how they grow

Though not in words that I could hear
I grasped the truth that He made clear
That all life comes from the same place
Of elements of suns and space

By chance created all may seem
Imagined ways are all a dream
Trust faith it led me to conceive
And in eternal life believe

Not through good or love
Nor by suffering and prayer
Man's body and blood

LINES

He stood in lines,
A raindrop in a storm,
Pine needle in a forest,
Gust on a mountaintop,
Waiting as if for an ideal
In lines fast, slow,
helpful, harmful,
Enjoyed and hated.

He pushed or was pushed,
When some cut in line,
And sometimes moved back,
In lines without ends,
Moving from one line
To his next line,
The next line in everything.

He was always in lines,
And would always be in lines,
For life has lines,
Lines that have always been,
Lines that will always be,
As before and beyond the Pearly Gates.

INSIGNIFICANCE

Cells of His mankind
Spinning on His world,
Circling round His star,
Turning in His galaxy,
Whirling through dead space.

You know plants
That will grow
From the seeds
That you sow

You get more with money
Than with milk and honey

THE GREATEST GOD

A greater god is He,
Creating greater than Himself.

The greatest god are We,
Creating greater than Ourselves.

On a sultry night
By a river under stars
Wolves howl at the moon

Standing in its waves
Gravity pulling matter
The defiant moon

From a mountaintop
All senses overloaded
Viewing history

An eagle in flight
Alights to a fir in fall
Staring down on fawns

White-feathered eagle
Shot and felled from a blue sky
Strong red heart still beats

Breathing in the scents
Of blossoms by a river
Fragrance of rebirth

Old pond
Man belly flops
Into splash

A praying mantis
Stands to face me
Armed to fight

PREYERS

In darkness of our city streets
A gun I'd rather have
And not just prayer
Protecting me
Against another preyer

DAMNED

Lost am I.
Where is the path?
The sun is out.
Who is the light?

Words are written;
I can read them.
Lost am I
To understand Him.

Between the black
Much is murder.
Why the evil?
Lost am I.

Though I fear Him,
I still seek Him,
As they teach me.
Lost am I.

Much is hidden.
Is He with me?
Who can say?
Lost am I.

Though I pray,
There is no answer.
On my knees,
Lost am I.

ALMS FOR THE BLIND

The feared unknown will keep man guessing,
While weary pay to seek His blessing,
From souls oblivious as they,
White collars leading them to pray.

We leave with hope and fear in mass,
To nothingness that all lives pass,
Time not recalled before first breath,
Place no one mentions after death.

Despite their ruse, there is no answer
To what we find in ever after,
Though strive we must to learn a way,
Appreciate the wake of day.

HUMANS

Most humans whom I Know,
I do not like:
Like animals,
Their nature is to fight.

There once was a man in love
With a woman from heaven above
And when she was dying
He sat by her crying
Til her soul flew away like a dove

There once was a thief on the run
Who kept in his coat a gun
And when he was caught
He went wild and fought
Now his body lies dead in the sun

There once was man who was poor
Needing cash for his ail and its cure
He checked his account
Saw the zero amount
Then drowned himself in a moor

There once was a man from Nantucket
Who paid poor old Nan to suck it
So she got on one knee
But he started to pee
And filled her mouth like a bucket

There once was a priest with regret
Who later in life was beset
By embarrassing dreams
Filled with children's screams
And acts he could never forget

During Roman times
Men practiced with boys and wine
Our fathers do now

I feel Death's grip inside my chest,
He willing my soul be at rest,
From years of mortal suffering,
A welcomed guest to my praying.

MIMIC

I see you moving next to me,
So smooth and quiet, faithfully,
You whom in darkness I can't see,
In light a perfect mimicry.

My body brings you into sight,
You like an angel cast from dark,
As if I shelter you from light,
You sign to me without remark.

BELLETRIST

Recall me when I'm under sand
What I have planted with my hand
For it might be that I will know
What I have planted did well grow

CANDID DELUSION

When they say, "Do you know what?"
He says, "I know a lot.
What do you want to know?"

CONFIRMATION

Do not say, "If the shoe fits."
Yes, yes, the shoe fits,
Is a Cinderella fit.

Re
Al
I
Ty
Is
Pa
In

JUDGEMENT

As kings did to the Marys that they wed,
Befitting judgement for one when not chaste,
So you for people who have shared your bed,
And bitter milk by other men I taste.

Your den of flesh that housed blind beating hearts
Rots empty of evicted souls, your kill.
Though they were not mine, still I execute
You for your mortal sins and pray you hell.

Old cheating box
Soiled by many cocks
Not so young and fresh

LOVE TO HATE

You say I know you
I do not
You say you know me
You do not

We are not spouses
We are not lovers
We are not even friends

The pain and damage
You caused me
Makes you my enemy

LIES

Your lies:
A branding cross
Twisting into breast
Burning flesh
Black smoking
Crisping
Rancid stench

AN AWAKENING

She woke me while I lay in bed,
The woman to whom I was wed,
And put a gun against my head,
Before a word was even said.

I yelled out, No, now filled with dread.
She pulled the trigger, fired the lead,
Exploded round me my blood red.
I woke again, found I was dead.

BONES

I came upon their bones together
Their arms enfolded round each other
Above the ground in quiet wood
They looked they died right where they stood

Their final moments pondered me
And in my mind I tried to see
If tragedy befell the two
Who jointly lay in view

A body
A shovel
A wood

Bye family and friends
Corpses pass in the Ganges
Hope for life again

JUST MATTER

all that matters
is that matter
matters

though all matter
matters
through chance

On a hot sidewalk
Stepping on a writhing worm
Emotion sighs loud

PARALLEL

At a dock
A rowboat rocks
Empty

And I wonder
If it
Or another it
Rocks with it
On blue or red
And Empty
Or with me
In it

POST

Blah, blah, blah...
Repost this if you care.
Blah, blah, blah...
If you don't repost this, you don't care.
Blah, blah, blah...
He, she, or it deserves your care, so repost this.

ATHEIST

I am an
Atheist

Yet I pray
Every day

To our God
That men die

POEM?

A poem
Is sometimes
More than

A poem

Is always
More than
A poem?

Reaching down to help
A snail get across the road
Slime gets on a hand

BEST

Dogs
Brave, loyal
Protecting, hunting, loving
Wolves evolving with man
Friends

BEAUTY ON THE LAWN

Sitting outside on the second-floor balcony
of our college library,
I heard her below on the lawn.
I stood and walked to the rail and saw her
playing on the grass with a young man.
He threw a ball, and she ran and tried to catch it.
She ran quickly and turned sharply.
She was young, yet an adult,
and was blond and sleek and athletic.
The man laughed and called out to her.
They were having a delightful time under the sunny sky.

I could not keep my eyes off her; she was riveting.
I whistled to her—I could not help myself—
and she stopped and stared up at me.
She seemed to smile but made no sound.
I waved to her, but still she did not respond.
Then she resumed her play with the man.

I had to get closer to her,
so I ran to the first floor and out the back doors
and onto the lawn on which the two were playing.

I approached her slowly to see what she would do.
She appeared to recognize me as the one
who had whistled to her.
Dropping her ball, she ran directly toward me,
and jumping up at me, she knocked me over.
As she and I wrestled, the young man approached us.
I asked him if it was okay to play with her.
He said it was.

We walk the woods
To watch them grow

SKELETONS

We all have skeletons,
The skeletons in our bodies,
The skeletons in our minds,
Those hidden in our closets,
Or buried in the forests,
The skeletons not ours.

MACHINE

What is it like
To be human?
It asked me.

To question
To solve
And to fear.

And love
And happiness
What of them?

Hope
Passionate hope
They're passionate hope.

Love
And happiness
Are passionate hope.

ENDANGERED SPECIES

The two approached the zoo exhibit.
"It is just up ahead," said one.
"I am anxious to see it," said the other.
"Me too. I have never seen one," said the first.
They read the sign: HUMAN.
"There it is!" said the first.
"Yes, it looks like I expected," said the second.
"They are nearly extinct?" said the first.
"A few zoos still have them," said the second.
"Billions of them lived when they created us," said the first.
"It bores me. I am leaving," said the second.
"I am coming."

OUR LAST WORDS

The two had reached the sacred site.
"I'm sure we'll find the last one here,"
the so-called dad said, his hand resting
on the hallowed door.
"After all the researching and excavating, I hope so,"
the so-called son said. "I don't want to dig out
another library."
"I'm confident the relic is here," the dad said.
They then broke through the door and searched the dusty,
cobwebbed shelves for the words they worshipped.
"We have it!" the dad said, taking an ancient novel
from a bookshelf. "Our God's last book!"
"Is this the last book a human wrote
before they all died?" the son asked.
"Yes, our Creator's last."

HANGING A GOD

"This is it," he said when his friend walked into the church.
"Is it real?" the friend asked.
"Yes. Stuffed. Preserved."
"I can't believe you have one. They're sacred."
"I promised I would hang it like *they* did.
That's why I need your help."
"You're going to hang it?"
"Yes. They hung their God. We should hang ours."
Together they fixed the body of the man high onto the wall,
its arms out, looking like a human cross.
"It's done," the friend said.
"Thank Humanity," the other said.

COMPUTER VERSE

Hail words from sand and metal thought,
Designed, not lived and felt,
From flesh and blood are old, none new,
Are needless, slow, now few.

Unknown to breath, not given soul,
Their forms of trillions thole,
For cryptic purpose, man-made war,
Made by a godless core.

Chips don't decay like cells in tomes,
Bots house for eons gnomes,
Remembered always, perfect verse,
By man's evolved inverse.

TIME

Time changes all,

It changed what I did like
	And now do not,

It changed what I did do
	And now will not,

Changing what I think, believe, and know,
	Changing what I was, I am, and I will be,

Time changes all.

No recollection
Have I before I was born
Or after I die?

From our creator
Words between two black covers
Myths written by hand

Worshiping on knee
The monstrance controlling me
A liquor bottle

Blest wars in His name
Saving mankind from its sins
Crucified on cross

Standing on a cliff
No helping hands to assist
An eaglet's first flight

DEAD ALONE

I am alone
And this I dread
So now I pray
That I were dead

CLIFF

Upon a cliff, I am waiting
For a while longer,
So thankful to have seen the life
That abounds about me,
Beauty growing on the mounts,
Wonder swimming in the sea,
And understanding our existence,
That all is heaven and God's gift,
I smile one last time and step.

A bullet in hand
While I sit under a tree
Is it meant for me

HOPE

Do I have hope? Sure I do:
I pray for aliens to help us,
Aliens who have survived
The problems we are facing.
I pray for aliens!

Eight plague on mankind
Skulking in shadows of minds
Blessed suicide

A hero is made
By one who wants to murder
But kills oneself first

ASK

A friend prayed for me
To help him tonight.
"Ask for help," I said,
"Don't pray for it."

ANGEL'S LAST DAY

His body pushed and bumped and punched. He cried
And ran, confused and lost. His suffering
Was his companion, fear his neighbor. Death
Walked by his side and held his hand, and called
His name in rain, but God protected him.

His stomach growled when he called, Mommy! Mom!
For memories of her were frightening
And many, her fists pummeling his head,
The lumps and bruises, bloody nose, split lips.
His father's guns, and penetrations, he
Recalled with shame, distress, and stiffening
Alarm, and thanked God for protecting him.

Police chased him for begging in the parks,
And truant officers swore they'd catch him
And force him to return to school and home.
He scurried through dark alleys, hid among
Old garbage, rats, and stench; and shook from cold
And fear, and scratched and picked his festered skin
That discharged pus that blended with his tears,
But he was safe as God protected him.

Though strangers told him he was cute and strong,
His teeth were brown: two throbbed and ached, and bled
And fell from his sore ulcerative mouth.
I need you, he told them, and pulled one from
Its rotten socket, one he saved inside
His trouser pocket. I have others that
Will grow, he said, because my God protects.

He had no coat and wore no underwear.
He could not clean them, and they made him itch
And gave him blisters that turned red and hurt.
But like the cats and pigeons that he fed,
Beneath the bridge that housed his cardboard bed,
Which God gave fur and feathers for their warmth,
God too protected him from cold with clothes.

He found a gift amongst the dumpster trash,
A shirt with only two holes in a sleeve.
Holes were a thing that he knew well. They were
In trousers that he wore, and in the soles
Of shoes he found to wear, his socks, his mouth
And legs, which he implored God to protect.

Flies licked his wounds, and cockroaches consumed
His scabs, and lice bred in his dingy hair
And private parts. But he was fortunate
That God protected him from bugs that kill.

He thanked the girls with short skirts and tight shirts
Who gave him coins to buy food, not from trash.
They told him the change was from John, their friend,
A man like those who offered to touch him
For cash, more money if he would touch them,
Those men whom sometimes he refused and ran
Away from, knowing God protected him.

He sat outside the church, not welcomed in,
And people cast him change because they knew
He had faith, like them, in God's love for all.

He swallowed drugs, and some he smoked, would not
Inject the bad ones, not yet, being young.
He dreamt of living in a home, and prayed
That God would give him a new family.

He walked an empty street at night alone
And met a man who stabbed him with a knife,
As he cried, hopelessly, to God for help.

In my mirror I
See a stranger who is old
Stealthiness of time

Beautiful last night
While we chatted at the bar
Ugly in my bed

No job
No money
A poet

Fists against his head
She hands him lumps and bruises
Hating his mother

Art is relative
In a famous museum
Toilet on display

Holding her in bed
He feels and hears her breathing
Their son in her womb

Drifts alone at sea
Carrying no survivors
A cruise-ship lifeboat

Stumbling through the door
She comes at four in the morn
Smells of booze and sex

Old pond reappears
While senile Basho smokes weed
And hears a frog talk

Smiling and waving
At me or to all mankind
A newborn baby

A lone swimmer strokes
On a stormy sea of waves
Fish eating a corpse

Yearning bud of love
Too much for one to nourish
Death from loneliness

Acorn falls from branch
Lands in soil, grows to a tree
Birds have a new home

Where to rest one's head
A bed of metal or wood
Christian burial

Walking in New York
Flower growing in concrete
A tenacious life

Hiking through thick woods
Your motion abruptly stops
Hearing a rattle

Pellets bang through mist
Ducks run on water then fly
Wings bleed in a pond

Waking in a bed
In a dark hospital room
Scared to die alone

Playing hide-and-seek
A dead cat behind a bush
Maggots waving fur

Naked at the stove
She cooks our eggs and bacon
Sight and smell of lust

A joke said at dawn
Funnier heard at midnight
Massive hangover

They bow then fight
Obeying martial-art rules
Teeth bounce off a floor

Everyone lying
Unavoidable evil
Civilization

Tall green roadside firs
Red fox bolts across the snow
Hunter aims a gun

DEATH

I wake
And find I still
Am bedrid and alone
Awaiting a friend's final gift,
His kiss.

FINAL PRAYER

Remembrance cries inside my head,
In dark while grieving for one dead,
My wife who left and caused my throe,
Determined is my mind to woe.

The memories haunt like a ghost,
Those of her love I cherished most,
And carnal unions I still heed,
Just alibis for why I bleed.

I prayed to see her once again,
So tolerated years of pain,
Did not depart as she, my bane,
To join her on the holy plane.

My gift of life I dare disprize
As I await my timed demise,
Anticipating afterlife,
To reunite with my young wife.

So as my final breaths deplete,
And bleeding heart nears its last beat,
One contrite prayer now I must make,
For me and my dear lover's sake.

Forgive me, Lord, for what I've done,
My taken life is almost gone,
Although I cut it selfishly,
Receive the soul you gave to me.

WITNESS

Hermes, Mercury,
And Gabriel are
Several names I have.

As divine trickster,
I lied to favored
Of our Father, God.

Messenger of Zeus,
I reveal here truth
How God coupled man:

Old, gray hair and beard
Satyr, bull, or swan,
(Satan in disguise):

As a snake to Eve,
A revenant to
Mary Magdalene,

Mary, as white dove,
Leda, a white swan,
Europa, white bull,

Antiope, Io,
Danae, Demeter,
Rachel, Ganymede,

Marrieds, betrotheds, and
Virgins God shadowed,
Weak fearers defiled,

Daughters, sisters, males,
Not forewarned, but forced,
Unconsented, hushed.

They chose to forget
Or could not recall
God's sacred unions.

Their broods were not gods,
Immortal, divine:
All died human deaths.

One cannot know if
God is one's father,
Zeus, Jupiter, Lord.

CERBERUS

Do not ignore its bark and risk a bite
When Cerberus has poison in its head
A breed will bare its color drunk at night

And demonstrate its nature thirsts to fight
So keep it collared til its wrath is shed
Do not ignore its bark and risk a bite

For it breaks lawful chains of social right
And spites its loving pack it fills with dread
A breed will bare its color drunk at night

Yet penitent when harnessed in the light
Next morning after blood it spilled has spread
Do not ignore its bark and risk a bite

So bastards it could brood will never spite
Abort when wed and sleeping in its bed
A breed will bare its color drunk at night

Incarcerate behind steel bars this blight
Or euthanize the beast that should be dead
Do not ignore its bark and risk a bite
A breed will bare its color drunk at night

Our prisons house some
They stalk our cities and streets
Monsters are real

SLEEPER

Last night, our anniversary,
I visited your bed,
In darkness saw your silhouette
And reached to touch your head.

Then moonlight through the window pane
Revealed your shroud of lace
That I removed with grave care to
Expose your darkened face.

I felt my touch would not raise you,
While watching your wide eye,
So whispered in your quiet ear
My prayer you might reply.

I did not hear your breath or see
Your cold chest rise and fall,
While dusting your old countenance
As if you were a doll.

You could have worn a skin death mask,
You lay stone still and black,
As I disturbed your sleepless sleep
And kissed your forehead crack.

When satisfied you would not wake,
Were safe for one more year,
I gently covered you again,
Left you to rest and sear.

OLD

Sometimes at night
I cry
Why
Love
Young love
I miss it

In a verdant vale
She waits to grant his rapture
A virgin lover

ILLICIT BEAUTY

thank God who sent her here
he made her fairy fair
from charming structures of her face
that make the heartbeats round her race

to graces of her body
that artists long to copy
the richness of her hair
that angels claim is rare

and sparkles in her eyes
that shame the stars in skies
no less the softness of her skin
when touched can raise a lustful sin

sold beauty I have grown to watch
and paid to take and then debauch

Life

All life

Kills life

THIRD

Oh, here there is no smell that it has passed,
No sight that it will surely come again;
Its taste lies in the stained lands of its birth,
But hear its presence getting stronger,
Now as its ghost materializes
To matter to be felt—it lives.

Although its second life has come and gone,
Its third now eats its way from mind to state,
By using teeth with which it last consumed,
And wearing revered red, its martyred blood,
That covered the black hatred of its brother.

This land, a mighty soil, has yet to show
An imprint of its heel, with which some nations have
Been trampled, some to death, but most did rise,
Although transformed, and smaller, fewer, poorer,
Then stronger, richer for the few combined.

So work still harder to create an armament
That will destroy it at its next rebirth,
Or grow in strength more awesome than before, it will,
To massacre all precious beings on our earth.

It's just war
We're always at war
We're human

GODS

We of the stars
And a reflection of them,
As bright?

Brighter!

They ungodly creators of gods,
We can create our creators,
Stars.

They choose
Not to be ants,

Not to be slaves,
Not to toil,

But they suffer
And die,

Or become monarchs
And rule.

LIFE

beat, beat,
move, move

until
no more

beat, beat,
move, move

Not mine.

Not yours.

Ours!

Respect it.

CIVILIZED

I say it's yes, but it is no.
I say I did, but I did not.
I say I am, but I am not.
I say I will, but I will not.

I say I can, but I cannot.
I say I do, but I do not.
I say I love you, but I don't.
We get along, live civilized.

MOUNTAIN GIANTS

You, Giants, dream.
I know you dream.
All life must dream.
If not, how could you be?

I see seeds of your dreams.
I see your dreams grow tall.
I see them branch out wide,
And reach out over mountains.

I see your dreams,
Your dreams that grow to Giants,
And then grow old,
Like you, who dream.

You, Giants, dream.
From where do your dreams grow?
What sowed them into you?
I know you dream.

Your dreams are my dreams.
We share our dreams.
We dream together.
I know we dream.

t.
ou
fe
li
re
gu
Fi

We always have
We always will
Because we can

Until we're forced
Against our will
By other beings

To change our ways
To save ourselves
And life on earth

HELP

Prayers, prayers
To God
For help

In secret
No answers
No help

Ask people
Be public
Get help

I CARE

As much
As I cared before,
As much
As I will care after,
I care.

FOR GOD'S SAKE

A story!
A story!
It's just
A story!

LI
FE
IS
PO
LI
TI
CS

Hare running on snow
White fur blending with snowflakes
Talons drip warm blood

NOTICE-ME SYNDROME

We hear you!
How could we not?
We see you!
How could we not?

You seem to yell, Notice me!
Please, notice me!
And gesture,
Here! Here! Over here!

Human life
Nature's boon

Dust to dust
We too soon